15 VIEWS OF ORLANDO

loosely linked stories

EDITED BY NATHAN HOLIC

This book is dedicated to the memory of Jeanne Leiby, a mentor and friend to many writers in the Orlando community, and the inspiration for the "15 Views of Orlando" project itself. Though she passed away on April 19, 2011, her work as an editor (at *Black Warrior Review*, *The Florida Review*, and finally *The Southern Review*), a teacher and mentor (at Alabama, Tennessee, UCF, and LSU), and a fiction writer (the collection *Downriver*), will certainly be remembered for many years to come. Each year, you can support her legacy and memory by submitting or donating to the **Jeanne Leiby Chapbook Contest**, sponsored by *The Florida Review* and the **University of Central Florida Foundation.**

CONTENTS

INTRODUCTION

STORIES

INTRODUCTION

NATHAN HOLIC

Here's a fun game: I name a city, and you try to picture that city as depicted in literature and film. Create a list of all the different stories that have offered a view of that city, and picture the portrait of that city painted by the various authors and filmmakers.

It's an easy game, too. Here, we'll start with a major American city: Chicago. Take a moment. Create a mental list.

What sort of images came to mind, and from which books, which movies? Did you picture the white city / dark city of *The Devil in The White City*, the immigrant meat-grinder of Upton Sinclair's *The Jungle*? Or did you skip ahead 100 years, picture the Caprini Green of *Candyman*, the suburbs of *Wayne's World*? The skyscrapers and offices of Joshua Ferris' *Then We Came to the End*? How many different authors have attempted to capture the personality of Chicago on the page or on the screen? How many have contributed to its legacy in literature, to its mythology?

Fun game, right? We'll try again.

Take another moment, and picture New York City as depicted in literature and film. Close your eyes. Heck, I could do my best to make this tough, and it would still be easy. I could give you a single decade—the 1980s—and you'd have no problem forming a list of books and movies which have left indelible "New York" images in your mind: Jay McInerney's *Bright Lights, Big City,* or Tom Wolfe's *Bonfire of the Vanities*, or Bret Easton Ellis' *American Psycho. The Muppets Take Manhattan*, even. Skip ahead a decade, and now *Sex and the City* immediately comes to mind. Pick any decade, and you've still got *Law & Order*. As a character in film and literature, New York is more often appropriated than Robin Hood or King Arthur.

Now picture Los Angeles. Picture Atlanta. Picture Boston, New Orleans, San Francisco, Detroit. Literature. Cinema. Television. I drop the name of a city—Baltimore!—and you're already thinking of the ports and the schools and the "Bodymore Murdaland" graffiti from *The Wire*. The American City used not simply as a generic setting, but crafted into a unique character every bit as memorable as the men and women populating the story, every bit as desire-driven and multi-dimensional as the men and women who have walked the city streets for centuries.

Easy game.

Now we'll try it one last time. Picture the city of Orlando. Make a list. What comes to mind?

Anything?

This thought has stuck with me for quite awhile, has—in fact—become a nagging frustration / question / goal for years, because when I close my eyes and picture the city of Orlando and its place in film and literature, I am left with this image: Carl Winslow happily herding his children through Disney World, pointing and laughing at some dancing Goofy or Donald Duck costumed character while Steve Urkel slaps along behind them. It is the cast of *Family Matters* enjoying a vacation episode in my fair city (or, rather, my fair metropolis), and even when I saw this episode as a middle-schooler, it felt horrible and phony. I'd been to Disney World several times, after all, and what I remembered most about the experience were the long lines, the heat and humidity from a full day outdoors (Urkel didn't even look like he was breaking a sweat!), the smell of the lockers where my father would store a cooler full of sandwiches for our entire family rather than spending God-knows-how-much at the concession stands and restaurants, the cheap plastic Mickey Mouse toy I'd beg my parents to buy for me at some edge-of-the-city gas station / souvenir shop combo...the hotels, too, and the claustrophobic feeling of cramming into a single room with my entire family of five...oh, I had a fantastic time as a kid, loved the rides, loved the sights, but it was nothing like the scenes from *Family Matters.* They'd given us a slice of Orlando—a slice of Disney World—without any honesty, and yet this is what I still picture when I think of the legacy of Orlando in books and movies? Steve Urkel?

So I'll breathe, and I'll take another moment to picture Orlando in literature and film. I'll build my list. And now I'm picturing a dozen other sitcoms with episodes real and imagined, all of them within the safe bubble of "theme park." Now I'm picturing ESPN the Weekend, Drew Brees on a float. Now I'm picturing Ellen or Rosie O'Donnell shooting a full week of episodes from Disney or Universal. I've got to be missing something, right? I've lived in Orlando for more than a decade, and there's got to be some book I'm forgetting about.

Zora Neale Hurston, maybe? But that still feels more "Florida" than "Orlando." And is there anything modern, anything that tackles the city in its contemporary form, the Disney World and Universal Studios theme parks *at conflict with* Downtown Orlando *at conflict with* Orange County *at conflict with* International Drive? Is there any film or book which peeks into the dark spaces, that is not simply satisfied with the façade of this international city, that knows that Parramore and the Coalition for the Homeless and the University of Central Florida and the Eyesore on I-4 and Wally's Liquors and the Mall at Millennia and Little Vietnam and Johnny's Fillin' Station and Bithlo and Metro West and the Orange County Convention Center and the Amway Arena (new and old) all co-exist to complete the personality of a city far more interesting and complex than the swampy X-marks-the-spot crossroads of I-4 and the Turnpike that Walt Disney pictured from his plane in 1963 as the future home of his theme park? Is there anything out there?

Deep breath.

And yet I picture Steve Urkel.

This was the genesis (silly as it might sound) for the "15 Views of Orlando" project, a collaboration between fifteen different Orlando authors, which hopes to provide that multi-faceted characterization of a city that we all—as residents, past and present—know has a lot of character, but which is too often acknowledged in the same bland and one-dimensional way.

For this project, we recruited authors young and old, established and aspiring; we found teachers and students, novelists and editors; the project is a work of fiction, but we found authors whose background or expertise comes not simply in fiction, but also in poetry, memoir, journalism, and blogging; the 15-part story takes place entirely within the Orlando metropolitan area, but some authors are lifelong residents, some are transplants, and some have moved as far away as New York, Chicago, and Los Angeles. The authors' views of the city alternate between dark and light, sad and funny, optimistic and cynical, epic and tiny, and are as scattered and (yes) schizophrenic as the city itself. Quite simply, the "15 Views of Orlando" project was created to be a literary portrait of the city, as well as a showcase of the town's literary talent.

But the word "portrait" sounds too static for what we wanted to accomplish, so we decided to make the project even more interesting. After all, we didn't want just a series of snapshots of Orlando's skyline.

Instead, "15 Views of Orlando" was envisioned and unveiled as a linked story unfolding over fifteen weeks: from the start of this project, our authors set about writing a long narrative that snaked and wound through the city, each installment focusing on a different location within Greater Orlando, each installment written to follow the last (with a character or event or image or moment always linking one "view" to the next). No, we didn't torture our authors by forcing them into writing a traditional story with a plot as clean as a sitcom episode; some characters take a bow and disappear, while others reappear again and again, their conflicts colliding with those from other stories. Like our city, all of these views live and breathe together, are dependent upon one another. And to fit the format of the Burrow Press blog, where the stories were originally published each Thursday in the Summer of 2011, each author had only *one week* to write his or her own 1,000-word installment in the story. Along the way, we asked our readers to post comments and add to our "Wish List" of places to visit. For the writers who chose to participate (and for your humble editor, who set these deadlines!), this quick pace and this constant feedback proved to be a unique challenge entirely different than any writing prompt or assignment we'd ever undertaken before. At the same time, the project became a source of community for the city's writers: one author encouraging the next, steadily mounting pressure for each new installment, every author sharing links and Facebook "likes" and promoting the latest story from all others, quick comments on the blog to show appreciation or pleasant surprise for where the story was heading and what was happening to characters or conflicts introduced several weeks before by writers who, when the project began, had never even met.

Fifteen views are certainly not enough to capture the city in its entirety, but we hope that, as you read each new installment in this collection, you can watch the personality and character and mythology of *our* Orlando grow. And we hope that, whether the authors included in this book are familiar or brand-new to you as a reader, the *15 Views of Orlando* story sequence offers a striking new portrait of the community of writers who call this city home.

1 TUNNELING

GENE ALBAMONTE

Town House Restaurant, Oviedo

I didn't realize how much I loved the guy until he was gone. Not only that, but I didn't even know if he was coming back in one piece. So there I was, thinking about my friend (infantry, Afghanistan)—who might as well be the brother I never had—while standing out in the back of the Town House Restaurant with a waitress named Eve, who gently balanced a cup against my lips and poured water into my mouth because I was too busy throwing a tennis ball against the wall.

"This is impossible," she said, rolling her eyes. "The ball is solid and the wall is solid." She said this as if I didn't know that already. I told her I wasn't stupid, despite the fact that I felt pretty stupid. I recently got laid off (editorial assistant, newspaper). I was 32 years old. I was a dishwasher. I moved back in with my mother.

Regarding the tennis ball: I was testing something Brian had told me twenty years ago, something called quantum tunneling. I had been throwing the ball since early that morning. I was waiting for it to pass through the wall. Brian had told me, when we were twelve, that a ball was made of wave functions and, according to quantum physics (and his father, who was a physicist), those waves can spill into and through a solid wall. Because of this, there was a chance that the entire ball could pass through to the other side if it was thrown against the wall enough times. So I wanted to throw it as many times as I could each day before getting back to work. Eve said she'd help out. She's a good person. I knew Brian would like Eve, too. She was sarcastic and silly and sometimes she flicked rubber bands at people just to get their attention.

I threw the ball until the diner opened for business, but nothing happened.

▪

The following morning, I went running before my shift. The good news: I was running farther and faster than ever, which I knew would make Brian proud. He was always there for me, always trying to make me a better person. Healthier, smarter, more optimistic. People would pay good money to have his optimism. He was the kind of guy who would cut the glass in half and say it was completely full.

The bad news: I was diagnosed with jogger's hematuria, which is what doctors call it when your urine is tinged with blood due to your bladder walls banging against each other like a couple idiots. When the doctor told me this, I thought of cymbals clashing together, like my insides were having a parade. Peeing didn't feel good when this happened either. Most people would stop running after being diagnosed with jogger's hematuria, but not me. During my runs, I pictured my bladder walls banging into each other, imagined the capillaries within them exploding like tiny fireworks releasing little sparks of blood.

The good news: the house Brian grew up in was on my route. The bad news: it wasn't the same house. His old house had been knocked down several years ago to make room for a larger, newer house. Some would see this as a tragedy, but, to be honest, the new house was pretty damn nice. I'd live in it. If I could have afforded it. If I still had a career, something that didn't involve the words "dish" and "washer."

Growing up, Brian and I had become so many things in that old house. Spies, novelists, detectives, musicians, boxers, songwriters, television hosts, ninjas, news reporters, scientists, directors, writers, architects. We'd roll out a sheet of butcher paper in his living room and design roller coasters with a pencil, drawing twists and turns as the room filled with the scent of all-day gravy—crushed tomatoes, garlic, sweet pork.

I ran down the old road that used to be just a blinking yellow light dangling like a citrine, but was now a full traffic light. I passed what used to be an empty stretch of grassland and was now home to a mall with a movie theater. The old was still mixed in, though. Near the Town House, there was still the plateau of one-story businesses rising above the sidewalks, and there were still places where you could catch the scent of cow patties scattered within a field bordered by chickenfence. If you went deep enough, you could still find a home turned into a tire depot with masses of black rubber stacked in the yard like mountains at dusk.

■

After our shift, we went out back and I threw the ball. We were out there till 2 a.m. I told her about the time Brian and I sat in his backyard and cut our palms with a knife and rubbed our hands together and became blood brothers. Then we were quiet for awhile until, looking at the tennis ball, I said, "Maybe you're right. Maybe this is impossible."

"It's fun anyways," she said, and then she sat down next to me with her legs crossed, looking up at the stars. If only he could see us. If only I could take a picture of that moment to show him when he came back: the two of us, Eve and I, outside the Town House Restaurant in Oviedo, the night heavy and black and blue, things chirping, not a human in sight. There was the thud of the ball and then there was the happy thought that pieces of the ball—impossibly small—were passing through the wall and into the diner and the idea that, one day, the entire ball could pass through if I just kept throwing it.

2 YOU ARE HERE

CHRIS WIEWIORA

Will's Pub, Downtown

It's been awhile since you've rolled all the way back on your Triumph's throttle and just gone. Brian said when he got back from his latest tour, right after debriefing, you and he would ride up to the Blue Ridge Parkway, both your left hands trailing in the wind, giving The Wave to all the motorcyclists in the other lane. As soon as you heard about Brian, you thought about leaving your helmet, gunning your bike, and slamming into something solid; but you didn't.

Tonight, you're speeding from Town House after pulling out the last tray of dishes, setting them on the shelf to dry, and wiping down the damp walls so no fruit flies would form overnight. When you were closing the dishpit, Eve slumped her hip against the wall, her apron slung over her shoulder, and a wad of tips rolled in her fist and she said, "What are you doing tonight?"

Of course, you had nothing. You don't have anything, really. You were planning to go back to your mom's and take a shower to wash all the speckled grime of the restaurant from your skin. Since you moved back home, you've not bought your own shampoo and soap, so maybe you can pretend you're not there to stay.

Eve said there was a show downtown at Will's. You knew the place, with dual pool tables and a photo booth in the front, and a stage with some floor space, and the bar wedged far in the back.

▪

And you remember this: You and Brian were in college. Brian was doing the whole degree-to-officer route and you were taking journalism courses while climbing up the ladder from internship to editorship at the *Orlando Sentinel*. But no matter what graveyard late-night deadline you had for stories and however pre-sunrise early Brian had to get up to do PT exercises, you made time to ride.

It was after a ride that you were in front of Will's where you two would sometimes go to grab a beer and catch a show of some up-and-coming band. A tipsy girl asked Brian if he wanted to meet her later at some club. Brian had on his helmet and he said, "What am I gonna do?" Then he mimed a two-step and swung his arms, but he never really danced. Still, the girl came up and grinded into his crotch. And right there on the street, this girl was taking him totally seriously. Brian stopped his jokey dance and just shook his helmeted head.

▪

And now you are here at Will's with Eve. There's a haze of smoke and red dots of cigarettes in the dark. The band is set up and plays.

A girl stands in the corner growling lyrics and she slides the strings on her Strat slung low at her hips; a guy with an Afro plucks on his bass while bobbing his neck to the groove; and another guy, an Asian with a thin mustache, brings it all together—he's right there in the middle, the stage presence—swinging his drumsticks like hammers: *pat, pat, pat* and then *crash*, along with a continual *thump-thump*, *thump-thump* of the kickdrum.

After the intro song, the drummer says, "Thank you. We're Fever." Eve says that they sounded like grunge and surf-rock. As they start their second song, you think of a soundtrack to the Tarantino movie.

Eve is inches from you. She's swaying in that way girls do. The way that is so sexy you don't quite know if they know it. Thankfully, you have a PBR in hand, so you have something to do. So you drink. Drink up. But it will be empty soon.

Eve is here. You are here. And your bike is on its kickstand out front. You think how the bench seat of a Triumph really is meant for two.

You're stalling. You're supposed to put your palm on Eve. Somewhere. It doesn't matter. Reach out. Do it. You can imagine Brian saying that, because he basically wrote that in his note:

Before I do the damage, I want to say I'm sorry. I don't really know who I want to say I'm sorry to for all this. I guess I'm just choosing you to tell everyone who asks. I realize that that's kinda fucked up. And I'm sorry for that, too. But, this isn't your fault. There's nothing you could do. "There's nothing you could do," that's how I've been feeling about all this. I don't really expect you to understand this (I really hope you never do understand where I'm coming from, and that this remains a mystery, because that will mean that you made it), but at the very least, for now, please just know that this is about me, and there's so much more for you, because your life—your life—is worth living. I believe you're going to get out there and do something. I mean, you can do anything. Anything! It's wild to think about your future. And this is it: I'm at the end, while you're right there at the beginning of everything.

3 IT'S A HOLLYWOOD SUMMER

J. BRADLEY

Fashion Square Mall, Downtown

I'm nursing my PBR tall boy at the bar when the stinger of a manicured index fingernail jabs my right shoulder. I glance over and see Val holding a black plastic shopping bag. "You're late."

"Sorry, there was a line. I got what we need, though."

"Good." I suck the rest of the PBR out like a 'neck, and slam the empty down. We step out of Red Star Tavern and into the Fashion Square Mall. I'm almost tempted to walk backwards and do a ghost tour routine whenever I see an over-tanned shopper or two staggering like blood cells, but we're here to avenge the past, not wallow in it.

We admire the resiliency of Radio Shack, ignore the death of literacy at the shuttered Waldenbooks, shrug off the faux-Times-Square vibe of Macy's before we finally stop in front of the Hot Topic.

"Barney, you sure you still want to do this?"

"Val, fuck yeah."

We step through the reverse horseshoe entrance and stop where there's enough space for Val to drop the plastic bag between us.

"Can I help you?" the third-stringer Suicide Girl behind the counter asks. We pull the official Star Wars lightsabers out of the plastic bag. The *whooom whooom* when the blades expand and move through the air is so accurate, George Lucas would weep in joy. I snap the Harry Potter cutout's neck.

"Yes. Don't take this personally." Val walks over and wounds Edward Cullen. We make it rain Nirvana, Korn, Green Day, Social Distortion t-shirts trapped in their plastic phantom zones all over the store. The counter girl kneels behind the counter, phone receiver in hand.

"Remember the Infinite Mushroom!" I howl, stabbing the assorted action figure boxes. And then I notice three cops, Tasers aimed. We're gonna be as hot as the summer of '98 soon.

4 FOLLOWER

DAN SINCLAIR

Waterford Lakes, East Orlando

Flip flop. Flip flop. Such noisy footwear. Swear I never wear these things, but it's hot. Fucking hate the humidity. I want dry heat. Like Vegas. One day. Nah, not Vegas. Be dead in a week. May hate Orlando's weather but doubt it'll kill me. I'm hurricane proof.

Shit. Where did Indigo go?

Humidity made me daydream again. Ha—Indigo *go*. That's funny. *Indigogogogogogogogogogo…*

"Grandpa!"

Ah, yes. Call me Grandpa.

She named me at our very first encounter. Didn't get a "Hello," or a "Do you need help," but was instead treated to a "How old are you?" Can't be sure because of dark nighttime sunglasses, but I think my answer of "29" got rolling eyes from the 22-year-old. She pressed her card against the little black box, opening the gate to my new apartment complex. I thanked my indigo-haired savior but only got a middle finger and "Move it, Grandpa" in response. Sometimes it's easy to feel invisible, and it was nice to be seen. It was there, watching her return to her old BMW and ignoring the honks and yells from my neighbors caught in traffic

I had caused, that I knew she'd be Indigo from now on. She never dyed her hair that color again.

■

Today, waiting by the hole in the fence, hands on hips, that lithe, multi-pierced firecracker's hair is lime green. She's not really mad. Bad days just get under her skin. It's bad today because of an incident at work (to which she refers to as "nerd terrorism" with no further explanation) mixed with the news of her roommate's cousin dying. Now she wants away from the bad crazy so she can get good crazy. That's why she's recruited good ol' Grandpa for a journey over to Waterford Lakes. "The Lakes"—as absolutely no one refers to it—features not only a wide assortment of retail venues and restaurants but, more importantly, several bars within walking distance. Plenty of good crazy to be had there.

On the other side of the fence, Indigo hands me a brown-bagged 40-ounce. Technically it's a 32 because local lawmakers think that eight more ounces would be excessive. Valid point.

I ask, "And what is this?"

She says, "The beginning."

She offers her drink and I clank mine against it in toast. We pour some out for our homeys.

I'm curious. "Was that for your roommate's cousin?"

She shrugs. "Didn't really know him."

"But he's dead."

"*She* barely knew him."

"What's his name?"

"Stan or David, maybe?"

I raise my 32. "To Stan, David, Brian, James, Eddie, Daniel, Scott, Peter, Frank, and all our fallen soldiers."

Her face brightens as we toast the soldiers we don't know. Then the rain comes. Hard.

We duck under the gas station's overhang. Amazing how thunderstorms still know how to sneak up on me. Torrential downpour. Thunder. The sky is almost black between the bouts of lightning. Next to me, Indigo dances to a song in her head, taking breaks between steps to chug her drink. The rain stops as suddenly as it started. Sunny, hot, and humid once again.

"Come on." And with that she's skipping across the parking lot towards Alafaya Trail. I walk briskly. I'm no skipper. By the time I reach her, she's already a sprinter lined up in her pre-race stance, ready to give it all she's got across multiple lanes of traffic. No crosswalks for Indigo and Grandpa. No adventure in that.

"Go!"

She's off and I'm right behind her. We're clear past the southbound traffic but have to stop in the middle to avoid the Northerners. One car doesn't think we'll stop and comes to a screeching halt, driver's hand holding down the horn. Indigo laughs and waves as we finish our journey to the safety of the sidewalk. Once there, I turn left to continue on under the 408, but not Indigo. She hops down in the trench off the road, right into the water.

I ask, "Change of plan?"

She says, "Always."

She wades through the mini swamp and climbs up the short hill toward the empty condos ahead. Fearless. Not me. I want no part of this swamp no matter how mini it may be. No gators, I'm sure, but snakes? She's already to the buildings.

Fuck it. A bold leap over the water and I'm after her.

Big yellow banners with frayed corners blowing in the wind let you know this place is "Now Leasing." Been hanging for over a year now but doesn't look like a single tenant resides here. Indigo stands alone in the courtyard in the center of the buildings. She's in her underwear.

She's pointing at me. "Clothes stay here."

She giggles as her panties come off. Funny. After each dye job I always joke the same lame joke, asking Indigo whether the carpet matches the drapes. Always get a sigh and a roll of the eyes but never an answer. Now the truth—there is no carpet. I try not to stare but her pasty bikini line works as a highlighter. My shirt comes off to distract me.

I ask, "Are we streaking?"

She shakes her head. Never knew her right nipple was pierced. "Streakers run. We're moving at our own pace."

I nod as if I understand. Don't know if I do but take my pants off anyway. She stands there in a *way*. Something I've never seen before. Proud and determined. So comfortable. *She's* not naked. I am. She wears this outfit better than any I've ever worn. Indigo has been many things before, but tonight, for the first time, she is beautiful. She offers her hand and I take it, ready to walk anywhere.

Attention Waterford Lakes shoppers, if you gander over into the distance you will see the approaching Grandpa and Indigo—he at his worst and she at her best.

Oh, we're not *completely* without clothes. *Flip. Flop.*

5 THE GENTLEST OF BENDS

HUNTER CHOATE

Intersection of Orange Blossom Trail & Sand Lake Road, South Orlando

A cluster of afternoon traffic rose up from the distance where the road was a shimmering black sea. Perkin hotboxed his cigarette and flicked loose the cherry in a burst of orange embers that ashed the sidewalk, then tucked the un-smoked portion into the front pocket of his t-shirt. He eyed the still roost of overhead stoplights and readied his NEED WORK, HUNGRY sign.

The lights burned from yellow to red and oncoming cars slowed to a halt. Idling engines clanked and sputtered dark fumes that sharpened the air. The faces behind the windshields were solemn smudges of pinks and browns. A family of tourists sat motionless in their white rental. The gleaming hood of a silver Mercedes captured the sky and rendered it small. The passenger's side window of a blue F150 pickup squeaked down. A feminine hand emerged from the open window and waved white as a sail. Perkin approached the fluttering.

"Spare some change?" he said.

A middle-aged blonde woman poked her head from the truck. She motioned toward the driver, a man with the graying buzz cut and wide shoulders of a retired master sergeant. "Talk to my husband."

Perkin stumbled to the driver's side, pushing his way through the heat-churn that ghosted up from the road.

The driver squinched up his eyes, ran them over Perkin before speaking. "You serious about getting work?"

"Never been afraid to sweat when there's a job to be had."

"Got any family?"

"Ginnie, my wife." Perkin's chin dipped. "And our daughter, Leah. She's nine."

The man glanced at his wife. They shared a look that ended with the faintest of nods. The driver thumbed open his wallet and papered loose a ten-dollar bill and a business card, handed them both to Perkin.

"Here's a few bucks to hold you," said the man. "You get to the address on that card by seven tomorrow morning, and we'll get you squared away with some work."

Perkin traced his finger over the business card—Jim Maddox, Buckhorn Plumbing. The address was on the other side of Orlando.

"I'll be there." He tucked the money and the card into the back pocket of his jeans. "Thank you for doing this."

The truck was already rumbling forward. A Triumph motorcycle swerved around Perkin as he shuffled back to the sidewalk. Once there Perkin faced the sky, and for a long time he trembled like a thirsty flower. He unfurled his fingers from around his sign and let the cardboard tumble to his feet. Then he dropped his gaze and scanned the ground. In his months of panhandling, he'd learned to track the hours of the day in shadowslide. He guessed the time as four in the afternoon.

Perkin crossed over Sand Lake Road and headed into the Mobil gas station. As the girl behind the register watched him move about the store, her tiny nose ring glinted like the loneliest of stars. He bought a pack of cigarettes to split with Ginnie and a handful of watermelon Jolly Ranchers for Leah. While the girl rang him up, he asked her about her nametag. She answered with the confidence of a faith healer, "Yes. *Michael.* Like the boy's name."

Perkin left the store and rambled across Orange Blossom Trail to the Heritage Hotel where his unemployment checks just covered the weekly rent on his tattered room. He passed the whores with their pirate smiles and mosquito-lumped legs. He ignored the twitch-headed boys who asked for a smoke. His shoes crunched over shards of broken glass that sparked from the blacktop lot, and he disappeared into the hotel's courtyard.

He found Leah alone in the room. The window unit droned musty air that rattled the blinds. Leah sat rigid on the bed. She waved a tiny hand, her eyes fixed to the thunder-stomp of wildebeests on the old television.

"What you watchin'?" asked Perkin.

"It's about Africa."

"Where's Mama?"

"She packed up the car and left."

"Say where she was leaving to?"

"I asked where she was going." Leah turned from the television and smiled, her tongue squishing pink where her top canine tooth was missing. "She said crazy."

Perkin snorted. "Probably went to stay with Mamaw and Papaw." His head shivered. "She just up and left you here?"

"I didn't want to go." The way Leah looked up at Perkin and paused made him think of a child ruler of an ancient kingdom. Her head tilted to the left and she added, "Someone had to stay here and keep you from foolishness."

Perkin's eyes flinched to the television. The image of a leafless tree cracked black across the blue hour. At first he didn't see the fowl. It was easy to miss, but perched near the top of the tree was the silhouette of some long-necked bird, the gentlest of bends among jags of barren branches.

6 A DRY FOUNTAIN

TOM DEBEAUCHAMP

Lake Keogh & Environs, East Orlando

Perkin sat in the mud on the bank of the retention pond across the street from Jim "Maddog" Maddox's McMansion, wearing the Baywatch-red bikini bottoms Maddog had leant him. Regardless of the sulfurous smell, Perkin wagged his flippered feet through the water and the cattails. His shoulders were strapped with Maddog's twin oxygen tanks, his forehead creased by Maddog's hard plastic mask. To the *tsk-tsk*ing of the neighborhood's sprinkler systems, and the roaring of mowers, blowers, weed-eaters and edgers, Perkin prepared himself mentally to start earning big-time.

The long ash of his Mustang cigarette fell through the heat and broke on the surface of the pond. Maddog, in a judo stance, performed a "cleansing scrape" with his brand-new Speedway Series 60-inch pitchfork. He puffed out his cheeks and held in his breath and dragged the Speedway slowly down through the air. Long strokes, Maddog said. With the wooden end, he drew a map in the mud of two small circles on opposite sides of a larger third. He drew a single line through the center of each, connecting them.

The tanks held two hours of air, Maddog said, not enough for dallying. Perkin's work would take him from this pond, through Lake Keogh, and all the way to the fountain south of Red Lobster. The wildlife, Maddog said, would not be abundant.

"We're still talking fifteen hundred bucks, right Jim?" Perkin asked.

Maddog knighted him with the convex side of the fork, one tap on each sunscreened shoulder. "Fifteen," he said. "That's right."

Perkin took the pitchfork, gave it a practice stroke from his sitting position, and felt more than anything like a joke was being played on him, but one that strategically was worth having played, one at the end of which the blinders would be removed and he'd be wildly rewarded. It was the sort of job he'd always wanted.

"Long strokes," Maddog said.

Perkin pulled his mask down, engaged his headlamp, and slipped from the heat and the sunlight and the long flat swampy-plain into the murk of the retention pond.

As Maddog had warned, the culvert between the pond and Lake Keogh was almost too narrow for the scuba tanks to pass. It was impossible to actually swim through the tube so Perkin crawled on his belly one corrugated ridge at a time, the dim egg of his headlamp bobbing just out of reach. The tines of the fork clattered against the aluminum and sounded all around him. Was it a gator crawling in his direction? Was it something worse? A few minnows darted as he fugued into the lake.

If he swam directly east, he would come to another culvert, and at the end of it would enter the lake in which the fountain floated. Maddog had described the blockage alternately as "a pile of clothes" and "a hornet's nest." He hadn't honored questions of the blockage's origins, however, and he hadn't thought it necessary to explain why this one fell within Buckhorn Plumbing's jurisdiction as opposed to that of the city or the Waterford Lakes maintenance staff. Maddog had only expressed the panic and the urgency in the voice of the Red Lobster's general manager, a friend of his, whose hungry, waiting clientèle, on stormy evenings, under dark skies, were wont to stare at the frothy spike and the splatter it returned to the wind-rough surface of the lake.

Uncurling now from the culvert and expanding into Keogh, Perkin stretches his limbs out like a star. His lips ache from clutching the mouthpiece of the regulator. His headlamp offers only a constellation of dust.

Though he's dived deeper, shadowier bodies than this one, he feels a kind of claustrophobia. Which way is east? A few larger pieces of paper drift by, the ripped logo of a Krystal hamburgers bag, a tourist map of downtown. A lone bluegill flutters out of the darkness to peck at the edges of each, and then disappears.

Perkin expected a different assignment, carrying pipe or twisting wrenches. Even as he tells himself he could use the money, the fifteen hundred dollars, he can't help feeling lost. He swims in the direction he feels he had been going, but how long is he supposed to swim? What if he's swimming in a circle? If he finds the culvert, how will he know it's the right one?

Even if he had a sort of premonitory power to tell him he was on the right path, that he would find the culvert and it would be the right culvert, his nerves would be no less shot. He would see himself flippering perfectly east through a series of tunnels at the end of which he would find, and with the pitchfork disperse, the orb of cotton and paper. The dark pond would be traded for a blizzard whiteness, a snow blindness in the midst of which he would catch a descending sparkle. He would see himself register it is as a human finger wrapped in dog tags. He would not think to read the name. He would find the hand to which the finger belonged and the arm to which it would be attached and so on. Perkin would see himself surface beside the fountain with the G.I.'s body in one arm, and its finger in his opposite fist. He would see himself swim to shore and walk the first few feet from the bank awkwardly in his flippers. He would see himself distract a policeman from a pair of nude youths and an angry crowd. He would be no more certain of his direction.

7 LIFTING VEILS

JAY HAFFNER

Albertsons, Oviedo

I left Florida fifteen years ago and, until now, I haven't been back. I didn't even wait until my high school graduation. Left the day before. Got in the car and drove north until the humidity broke and I could roll down the window and not feel like I was breathing through a heavy wool blanket. By the time my senior class was listening to speeches about how their futures were right there in front of them, I was driving through Southern Tennessee, climbing the great Smokey Mountains, hugging my future as close as I could.

Presently, I have a 12-year-old son who's joined me on my return to Oviedo, a growing suburb to the northeast of Orlando, just far enough beyond the shadow of Mickey's ears to not be considered touristy but still close enough to know that he's there, looming. Jack thinks the reason for this trip is to visit my brother Jim (Uncle Maddog to Jack).

But that's not really the case. His mother, my wife for the time being, is fucking the neighbor. Though that would be disturbing enough if it was Paul or even Tina (their marriage is nothing to write home about), I'm sorry to say it wasn't. Instead it was Brucey, Paul and Tina's 17-year-old son. Naturally, this is a volatile situation no 12-year-old boy should be part of. My protective instincts kicked in and we hit the road.

"What is that?" Jack asks, the bill of his baseball cap resting against the passenger-side window.

"A farm. The Duda family has owned land around here a long time. Celery, lettuce."

Jack rolls the window down as we drive by, and he pokes his head into the blazing breeze.

"It smells bad. Where are the oranges?"

I want to explain to Jack that perception and reality are never the same. When I told him we were driving to Florida, he immediately thought about magic, happiness, the smell of oranges. The reality is that any magic that Oviedo once held has been drowned out by Wal-Mart Supercenters, Home Depots, expansive subdivisions...The only smell filling the car is exhaust.

The perception was the same with my marriage, too. To the outside, it seemed as if Molly and I were magic. When we walked into a room, we brought with us a cool Spring breeze softly scented with the smell of citrus, mythical as Florida. The reality is that our marriage had been on a slow but gradual decline for some time. It was easy to convince people we were happy and in love. In fact, when we had the chance to leave our own eroded reality for a few minutes, we almost believed it ourselves. But underneath perception lies a truth only visible if one has the courage to lift the veil. Perhaps

Molly's affair was a courageous act, finally lifting the veil and exposing everything we weren't.

"When I was your age, this road didn't exist," I say, as we pass a shopping center and an upscale sushi restaurant.

I drive up Red Bug Lake Road and approach Alafaya Trail. I smile at how "small town" Florida those names are, how unbefitting to the current state of Oviedo. I'm reminded of Sunday morning breakfasts at the Town House diner, afternoon swims out at the lake with Maddog.

What I really want is for my son to learn everything about me before his veil is lifted, too. It's only a matter of time before he has to deal with the shame of his mother, the failures of his father, the gross reality of who we are and what we've become. My only wish is to build as many perceptions of me into him as I can; a deep crevasse drilled through the center of his reality, filled with romanticized stories of my youth.

But it seems as if my past is crumbling along with my present. The old Albertsons grocery store—where, as a child, I rode the cart while my mother shopped, where I worked through high school—is now nothing more than a shell of what it once was. The Albertsons is gone, its adjoining stores closed as well. The great white building, once a pearl of neighborhood commerce, is tainted and ashen, the parking lot littered with trash. The centerpiece of what was to become my son's perception of his father is now a bombed-out building caving in on itself.

"Dad, this is sad."

"It didn't used to be," I say, driving around to the side where I find the words "Pussy ain't free" slap-dashed in graffiti across the wall.

I take Jack by the hand and we walk to the front entryway. I want to show him the parking spot where I unloaded a lady's grocery cart on my first day of work and took a two-dollar tip, not knowing that it was strictly against company policy to do so. I want to show him the side door where, years later, I snuck cartons of cigarettes to a waiting friend who then sold them at school, knowing full well *that* was against company policy. I want to take him inside the store, behind the produce department, and show him where I kissed my first girlfriend back in the ninth grade.

"Can we go over there?" Jack asks, pointing to a shopping center on the other side of Alafaya Trail, one filled with shops, restaurants, life.

The windows are dusted and dirty, but it takes little effort to see inside the old Albertsons. The shelves are toppled against one another, piles of busted rock and twisted metal littering what used to be the drug department. A newspaper floats past my feet, today's date and the headline FOUNTAIN MYSTERY, but it's come from somewhere else; the newspaper machines here are all empty.

"I used to work here," I say to my son.

"I'm sorry," he says, laughing as he kicks an empty beer can against the wall. "Dad, I'm hungry. Can we go?"

The Florida air feels thick in my throat. The cool A/C of the car awaits, so I shuffle Jack back into the front seat.

"Where to now?" he says.

Good question.

8 DECONSTRUCTION

ASHLEY INGUANTA

Little Vietnam, Downtown

The Beginning is a bottle, a brown-bagged 32-ounce I gave to Grandpa on the day I swallowed him whole. He thought he could outdo me, jumping across the lake like that. And when the Waterford shoppers got angry at us for taking off our clothes, I tugged my nipple ring and made a dress to wear out of Water and Earth. Then I folded Grandpa into a small rectangle, thin as a sheet of paper, and slipped him in my pocket as I walked down Colonial.

We passed the gold sellers and pawn shops, and right when we passed our favorite gold guy, the one who's spray-painted 14-karat, Grandpa said he felt cozy in his old age, in his invisibility. I said, "Soon you'll be 30 and you'll become different." He didn't disagree. Our silence became nothing but air, waltzing. That's when I decided to take him out of my pocket, slide him down my throat. I wanted to take him apart, see him in his smallest form, and place what I loved about him inside of me.

So if The Beginning is a bottle, then The End is a crow. I don't tell this to anyone—it's my secret. I've already spilled too many of my secrets, let the world know who Love is and how Love and Scar Jubilee and Broken Bone Baby were the same to me, once. *I want my secrets back*, I say to Grandpa, who is still inside of me. He is too pissed off to reply. I don't blame him.

But I am there now, on Mills, in Little Vietnam, so I don't care that Grandpa isn't talking. I choose to stop here because this is where I learned Love is not a scar or a broken bone. I think about this, all the learning I've done, as I walk past the Asian Farmer's Market and Little Saigon and the big graffiti Jesus near Pho88. I think about asking Jesus to save me, but I'm done with that—building things up, finding new hope. All I need is here, in front of me. I think about my roommate's cousin who died, how we don't even know his name for sure. *Name*. What is mine? *Indigo*. I don't want anyone to know my name or my secrets.

I don't even want Grandpa in there anymore, tumbling in my stomach, getting that close-up view of my insides, so I stick my fingers down my throat and throw him up. He runs away, still naked. *Flip flop*. I go into the Chevron and a homeless woman asks me for some money and I give her a fifty. I buy myself a can of sweet tea the size of two fists, stacked. I walk outside. I see myself, four years ago, before I wrote down my secrets and had others read them: my hair is bleached blonde and I am standing smack in the middle of the road. I go over to my 18-year-old bleach-blonde self and grab her by the shoulders, shake her hard. I shake her so hard she falls apart, her heart and lungs and spine tornadoing outward, sticking to anything and everything in Little Vietnam—the Lollicup, the video store. Years later, when the 18-year-old girl falls apart for good, when the air is a holy mess of Nothing and Never-Will-Be-Again, I understand what's in store will be moon-heavy and boombox-bright. I will take apart my life, tug at its roots.

Change of plan? Grandpa will say.

Never, I will tell him.

I will lie. I will throw him a bone and he'll go, running like the shadow of a bird, into the bruised night.

9 CONS

CHRIS HEAVENER

Wekiwa Springs, Apopka

She pulled out a slim composition notebook the minute I picked her up from the airport. We headed west on the 528 toward I-4. She flipped to her list.

She said, "You're not going to like it. There's not a lot of pros. Actually it's mostly cons."

I told her to read it anyway. Cons first.

"It's an angry place. I read on some news website last night that Orlando is the angriest city in the nation. Did you know that?"

I didn't.

"Apparently it is. Doesn't surprise me. Put a bunch of underpaid employees in heavy synthetic animal suits in 100-plus degree weather and force them to be not only cordial to entitled tourists but goddamn *jolly*? Of course you're going to have a disgruntled population."

I reminded her not everyone works for Disney down here. I asked her what else.

"The place sprawls like a son of a bitch. You have to own a car to get anywhere. And it's got one of the worst rated public trans systems according to *US News and World Report*."

Anything else?

"Plenty. It's powerfully segregated. The black population has very little contact with the white population."

And.

"The public education system is horribly underfunded. If I moved and got a job here, it would be a constant battle with the school board to get even the most rudimentary of teaching supplies."

What else?

"It's home to, and built upon the foundation of, one of the most exploitative and deceptive corporations in American history."

Merita Bread?

"Walt Mother Fucking Disney World!"

I said c'mon. Disney is like thirty percent of what this place is really like.

"The city's existence is still predicated on it."

We grew quiet as I exited the 528 and took the slow turn on the overpass and merged onto I-4, splitting the heart of the city: the opulent downtown high-rises to the east and low buildings of the Parramore district to the west. There was traffic. She wrote that down as another con. I asked if there were any pros.

"Plenty of swimming pools."

I knew she loved swimming and there wasn't a lot of that in Tucson. I told her I was taking her to swim someplace special.

"If we're going to one of those pee-filled water parks, then I'm going to be irate."

I said it was much better than that.

"Good. Those things are MRSA infection factories."

We drove north. Commercial buildings became sporadic as we drove through Altamonte, Lake Mary, and faded away altogether when we hit Sanford. Cypress and pine trees walled the interstate. She gasped as the trees disappeared and gave way to the St. John's River.

It runs from Jacksonville all the way down to Okeechobee, I told her. I was hoping she wouldn't look west of the interstate, not even a half-mile downriver, where a giant nuclear power plant hunched over the river's edge, slopping up water. She did.

"Of course." She clicked her pen, wrote down another con.

I asked if there were any more pros.

"You're here." She smiled at me, then looked back to the river.

I wanted to ask if this was a big enough pro for her to pick up stakes. But I didn't. She'd just arrived, and I didn't want to put her on the spot. It might've set a strange tone for the whole visit. If I'm being honest, I was scared of what she'd say.

■

We pulled into the gravel lot of Wekiwa Springs park. It was early in the morning, also a weekday, so the lot was mostly empty. She struggled to pronounce the name of the place. Wah-kye-wah, I helped her out.

She *ooh*-ed and *ahh*-ed at the thick vines and Spanish moss dominating the Cypress trees. The city cranked up her heat. She vented by jabbering. But nature quieted her, it calmed and slowed her breathing. She wouldn't admit it, but I saw she enjoyed just getting out of the car. She brought her comp book with her anyway, just in case.

I led us through a trail, pointed out banana spiders and deer tracks.

The trail was well-worn and clear. Most people take that trail to cool off at the cliff jump on weekends. I wanted us to be alone, so I made sure we came out here first thing.

The fat man ahead surprised me, standing in the middle of the path, holding something up close to his face, studying it. He was alone. A dry twig snapped under her foot. The fat man dropped whatever was in his hands and looked at us. I waved at him and we advanced. He didn't wave back. Gym trunks hung like curtains around his waist, a stained tank top cloaked his gut. Sunset-tinted glasses distorted the sides of his face.

He stood still and heaved quietly as we walked past him. I could feel him on us. On her.

The brush got thicker on the trail. Invisible spider webs clung to armhairs and eyebrows. She was getting distressed. I told her we were close. The trees cleared to a cliff. Three stories below, a blue-black spring surged. I took my shirt off, bundled my wallet, keys, and phone inside it.

"How deep is it?"

Fifty feet? A hundred? I didn't know. People came out here with scuba gear and dive lights all the time. She said it was beautiful.

I noticed something change in her. She mashed her eyebrows together at most things, as if nothing in the world passed her scrutiny. That inability to accept any transgression, even the slightest, had worn a wrinkle in between her eyes. That was melted away now. I wanted to ask her if this place was a big enough pro. I was still scared. I jumped instead.

Breaking the surface was violent and expected, but the cold setting in was like walking into a dark room you've never been in before. Disorienting, unfamiliar, emptying, like there's a window in that darkness that could vacuum out everything you think you know about yourself.

I surfaced, looked up at her, and smiled. I yelled for her to jump in. She said no way. She was smiling. I want to remember her that way: smiling. But I'll never be able to do that.

One look on her face has erased any others from my memory: the look of walking into that dark, unfamiliar room. A look bloated with the knowledge that every part of who she was would soon be extracted and dissolved without explanation.

It was the look of an animal caught in a trap, as the fat man materialized from the trees and dragged her into the woods.

10 THE LITTLE LITTLE DEATH

JARED SILVIA

The Booby Trap, Winter Park

Kevin's car always had little lights on in the small place between the speedometer and tachometer. One was a little engine, and the other looked like an eight on its side.

We had left Wekiwa Springs because it was getting dark, and we were down to just one 32-ounce beer. Kevin was driving with one hand on the wheel and the other around the neck of the bottle between his legs.

"You know that sinkhole over on Denning in Winter Park?" he said.

"I didn't know there was a sinkhole on Denning," I said.

"One day in '81," Kevin continued, "fucking ground opened right up and swallowed a house, a pool, and a Porsche dealership."

"I like Porsches," I said. I started thinking about my favorite Porsche, a red 928. They were expensive.

"They busted the dude who owned the car place trying to pull those Porches out of the water with a tow truck in the middle of the night."

"That is weird," I said. "Why would he do something so weird?"

"There was cocaine in those cars."

"Oh, I see," I said. That made sense. People like cocaine.

"Fucking cocaine," said Kevin. He flexed his fingers hard against the steering wheel and they made a little squeaky sound. "If I could get some goddamned scuba gear, I tell you what I'd do. I'd get down in there and get me some of that Porsche cocaine."

"But you don't have any scuba gear," I said, and looked out the window at all the plazas.

"If I did...well, that sure would be something," said Kevin. He took a big drink of his beer, and then wiped his mouth with his shirtsleeve.

"I need to see some girlies shake their asses," he said. "We're going to the Booby Trap."

▪

The Booby Trap was a club with two knocker-shaped domes that you could see from the highway. It wasn't actually called the Booby Trap anymore. It was open Tuesdays.

Kevin parked out back by the fence. He didn't like his car to be right up front.

Inside, the air was sweaty and hot. It was thick, and it made my throat tickle. There were only a few people inside. There was a group of cops all huddled around one table. A girl was dancing near their table, looking sort of confused. The bartender was checking her cell phone. Another girl was at the end of the bar wearing short shorts and a glittery cowboy hat, playing video poker.

"I'm gonna get a girlie," said Kevin, surveying the room.

"Alright, let's go find a girlie," I said, but Kevin shook his head.

"I think I should go by myself. Why don't you go over there?" Kevin pointed to an empty booth on the other side of the bar.

I sat down in the empty booth and thought really angry thoughts about Kevin. He never considered what I wanted. He always did what he wanted. Maybe I wanted to talk to girlies. He didn't care.

"You don't look like you're having any fun, honey."

A lady was leaning over the back of the booth. She was wearing silk.

"I'm fine. It's really nice in here. All the strippers look very hot."

"Mmm. You like hot strippers?"

"Yes," I said, "I like hot strippers a lot. My friend Kevin is over there, and he and I both like hot strippers."

"I'm not worried about your friend Kevin," said the lady, winding her way around the booth. She stood in front of me and pulled a cigarette out from the pocket of her silk robe and lit it. "Tell me what *you* like."

"I like it when…" I said, and tried to think of something really hot.

She pressed her boobs together.

"Do you like those?"

"Yeah, they're really good."

"Mmm. How about this?" She lifted her light garment and showed me her backside.

"Yeah, that's good too."

She swayed in place, which made me think I was supposed to say something.

"My friend Kevin really likes it when a girl shakes it right in his face," I said. "I'm allergic to cigarettes."

"Tell me more about Kevin," she said, tapping her ashes away.

I coughed. "Well, Kevin and I are really good friends, and he brought me here tonight so we could look at hot strippers, and…"

"You like girls, right?"

I nodded. She sat down next to me and placed her cigarette between her lips.

"I think I know what you'd like," she said, and put her hand on my upper thigh. She felt around.

"Hmm," she said, rubbing up and down. "You're packin' heat, honey."

"That's my inhaler," I said.

"Oh," she said, and moved her hand to the other side. "What about that?"

"Oh, that is…" I said.

"I know what that is," she said.

"Oh," I said.

She moved her hand up and down against it, and looked over her shoulder at the bar. She shifted her cigarette between her fingers.

"Don't tell no one I did this, alright?"

I nodded, maybe. It was hard to think. I was feeling warm, and sort of good and itchy all over. She was rubbing, and I was licking my lips like you're supposed to.

It felt so good, and I was feeling excited.

Then I sneezed really hard. It was right at her.

She was looking down at her tube top, which was all wet. I was pretty embarrassed.

"Sorry I sneezed on your titties," I said. Then I got up and looked around.

Kevin was waving at me from over by the bar, so I walked over to him.

"Check out that girl," he said, pointing to the girl on the stage. She was rubbing her backside on a big plastic pole. "She's an adjunct at SCC! I'm going to the champagne room with a professor! Right after this dance!" Kevin was really smiling, and soon I was smiling, too.

We were both smiling together.

11 HEART

LINDSAY HUNTER

Florida Hospital, Downtown

The man griddling pancakes don't look me in the eyes when he fills my plate. His eyes drift upward toward my hairline, skitter down to my neck, I feel for the man, I ain't easy to look at.

I feel for the man, that's one hallway, but down another hallway I watch myself beat the man with my tray until his head's a broken gurgling pie.

My momma always said I got a head shaped like a heart. Not like them cartoon hearts bitch girls draw about other boys in their notebooks. Like the real thing. A pumping chambered ugly of a muscle not meant for no light of day. Guess that means instead of brains I'm all blood. Guess that's why I ain't ever been scared of blood. It's warm like I'm warm. It pools thick and gorgeous and don't step in it less you want to make a painting of what you done for any passing bitch to start hollering about.

Rest of me's just flesh. Mounds and folds of flesh, rubbing against itself, slick like a tongue through a mouth, when I feel rotten I pretend all that sweat is blood, my insides pouring out, the sky above me narrowing to a speck till there ain't no sky and there ain't no me.

But then I always wake up, my head and heart pounding, clobbering me all to shit.

I ask the pancakes man does he know if there's pie, he points his spatula away from himself, I turn in that direction but he is pointing at the soda machine. I feel that spider I get in my belly again, that prickly thing. I close my eyes, push the corner of my tray into my belly till it hurts and past till it hurts, till the pain feels normal and that spider's a goner.

It ain't the man's fault, the spider, I got to keep reminding myself it ain't people's fault.

A lady in scrubs rings me up. Tonight it's pancakes, a waffle, curls of bacon, a dish of macaroni and Velveeta, a good size fluff of scrambled eggs, a wrapped sandwich for later, a salad I ain't going to eat. A wedge of cake, red with white frosting. The lady's flesh is the color of honey, flecked with tiny dark freckles. I wonder is something wrong with her, that honey color and everything, then I realize I like it, I like that color, I like this lady in her shirt of colored cats, I say, You like pussycats, huh? but the lady says, No, like I just asked her did she like eating babies, holds out her hand for the money.

Another thing about me is, I got a real hard time showing my true emotions. So inside me there is a roaring, I am the roaring, it shreds the lady before me, it hangs her by her cat shirt, her tongue pink as a lozenge, but outside me I thank the lady, ask her could she just keep the change.

I sit way in the back of the lunching room. There's only a few other people here, a crying lady crumpled over her tea, two thugs in white uniforms, holding them plastic spork things in their skinny fists, a man watching a little girl fingering dimples into her mashed potatoes. I don't want none of them watching me eat.

From the back of the room I can see out the windows, the sun finally gone, a jagged pink-orange stripe all that's left of the day, like someone melted a taffy and made a nasty smear. My mouth is watering, I want to jam all that food in my mouth at once, even my napkin, even my straw and cup and utensils and packet of salt, I want to go over and eat the mashed potatoes off the girl's plate, suck the bits off her fingers, try not to bite down.

I wonder does anyone else ever feel this way. Does anyone else ever feel like the wrapper to the taffy.

When I'm done I use the pads of my fingers to get the crumbs, I don't want to leave nothing behind. *Graso*, one of the thugs says, sniggers into his hand.

Momma and I at Wekiwa Springs. Me eating a Dole Whip, licking it off my forearm, my elbow, mistaking salt for sugar. The man Momma was with slapping the cone from my hand, That's enough, Fatty, he said, Momma laughing, Momma telling me to go off by myself for a while. The water lapping quietly, the light in the trees.

Blood in my heart, blood in my head. It's a comfort sometimes to think about all the waves of blood lapping just under the surface, all around me.

The thugs get up, still laughing. Down one hallway, I laugh along, down another, I—

12 SOMEBODY TO LOVE

PHILIP F. DEAVER

Tom & Jerry's, Winter Park

"Brucey?" I say to my beautiful eldest daughter, Molly. The music's caving in my head, but it's my era so I guess I love it. Grace Slick, "Somebody to Love." There are tall tables in this section, and we're sitting across from one another. Molly's a wreck. She's been crying. We're waiting for her sister, who gets off at eleven if she doesn't have to close. "Brucey?"

"I know," Molly says, teary-eyed, leaning forward so I can hear. "He's very cute."

She's smoking, and I really can't stand the thought of it. I remember when she started, years ago. All her friends were, so she did. Now it's got a hold of her. It's got her by the throat, in fact. She's 31 and the voice is basically gone. She's the one who suggested Tom and Jerry's, an old-school bar on a dilapidated stretch of 17-92. She'd have preferred Will's Pub, but this was closer to my place. It's thick with smoke, full of twenty- and thirty-somethings at scattered, tall tables like ours or just standing around. The walls are reddish brown, worn-out, dim, and gloomy. At a lower table in another part of the room, there's a 40-ish guy with a gal half his age sitting on his lap. There's a girl with blue hair and a really lousy tattoo on her upper arm standing with three guys watching the local news on a flat screen above the bar. It's closed captioned, so they're watching close. There's random dancing.

Brucey is a 17-year-old neighbor kid Molly's been fucking for some reason. She and her husband live in Chattanooga. For several years it seemed all was well, but the quiet from up there had recently grown ominous. Early this morning her husband somehow figured stuff out and left with their boy, my grandson. Molly figures they're down here in Florida. Her husband's family lives over on the east side.

Molly's son, Jack, is only five years younger than Brucey. I'm speechless. There was plenty of anarchy in our house when Molly and her sister were growing up, but nothing like this.

"It's a mess," she says. She's kind enough to blow smoke some other direction. "Don't say anything. I screwed up, I know it. Don't say anything." Her hand is raised, palm out, in the stop signal. The music's real loud.

I call to her through the din, "So what now?"

"I know, right? Don't *say* anything, I told ya."

Right then, Eve walks in with some guy. She gives me a kiss on the cheek, then gives Molly a big hug, then introduces the guy to Molly with some kind of sign language. Which she translates to me by yelling over the music: "It's Brad!" she says, pointing. "He's an editor at the *Sentinel*!" She laughs. "He *was*, I mean! He works with me at the restaurant. *Temporarily*."

Brad reaches between my daughters to shake my hand. I can see he's older than Eve, closer to Molly's age. He's got a wise, tormented look in the eye. Compared to others in the room, I think he might be okay for Eve, not that there's such a thing as dating anymore. A pitcher of beer arrives—so now we've got Grace Slick and Pabst Blue Ribbon, I'm not kidding.

I need to get air. I tell them I have to make a call. I take my beer and find the exit through the noise and white nicotine fog.

Outside there are tables, but they aren't far enough away from the smoke and noise. The parking lot has a smattering of cars. North and south are other parking lots—surfaces mismatched and cracking up—used to be lots and driveways for other places, Hardee's, a U-Haul dealership, used cars. Those buildings are all gone. This is the lone survivor, straightforward concrete block, no windows to speak of, established the year I was born, so says the sign out front. I'm pacing in the parking lot, beer and phone. I set my glass on the asphalt and speed-dial my ex-wife, Meg. She picks up immediately.

"Well?" she says.

"Okay," I say to her, "so I talked to her, and it's not too bad."

"That doesn't sound good, Ned," she says. "What's that mean?"

"Nobody's dead or anything."

She hisses real fast, "Listen, my friend, do not bullshit me one more moment—tell me what's going on."

I welcome the opportunity to let it out. "She's apparently been seeing somebody, and somehow it came to light, and Jake left and took Jack. She thinks he came down here, so she drove down in the Jeep. She wants to…" An ambulance whips by, lights flashing, no siren.

"She wants to what."

"I don't know, catch up to Jake and explain or something."

"Explain!?"

"Or something."

Brad comes out of the bar and climbs on a really gorgeous Triumph. It pops to life. As he goes by, he says, "Nice to meet you." Once he's on the street, he makes a statement with the throttle and totally drowns out Meg for fifteen seconds.

When the bike's gone, she says her little speech again: "What's to explain?" Except now she's crying. "Everything's gone to trash. I really can't stand it."

"Look, nobody died."

"Shut up, Ned. Everything's trash. It's unrelenting." She cries hard for a few moments. I pace and drink in the dark parking lot. It sounds like she's really losing it. I wait. The night's close and warm. Finally she starts to clear herself. I hear Kleenex. "Evie get there?"

"Yeah, just now."

"How does she look?"

"Great. They both look great."

"Everything's just great, isn't it," she mumbles, Kleenex at her nose.

"Come on over. You'd feel better if you saw them. You know where this place is?"

"Shut up a minute."

"Across from the old Honda dealership."

"Jesus, Ned, shut up."

On a pole above this bar, around forty feet in the air, all by itself with no explanation at all, is a sort of pink, bombed-out '58 VW, a real one, with the driver's side door flapping in the wind.

"It's good to see them together," I tell her. "Still the same kids, honey. Oh, and they're the same height. When did that happen?" I always try to sound cheery with Meg. She's always got that drastic sound in her voice, like pending thermonuclear war.

"Ned," she says, "please please please please..." Meg's a lit major. We've been divorced a longtime.

"Okay, look, you should come over," I tell her again. "I could leave—it'd be all clear," I say. "It's just five minutes from your place, get a move on. The girls'd be blown away if you showed up. You'd love it. There's a gas mask in the basement. Remember, in the Halloween box?"

Cars click by on 17-92. It's a concrete street, so the radials register a clacking sound on the tar seams. It's high summer, bright moon, a night-hawk up there somewhere. The driver's side door on the VW makes a yawking sound when it moves in the wind. Needs grease. Don't we all. Meg's still crying.

"Shall I let the girls know you're gonna come over?" I stand still, drink the last of the beer. I wait. No reply from the ex. It's me, I know it is, something about my approach. "Okay, babe. Bye." I hang up on her.

Right then Eve comes running out of the bar. She spots me under the flying pink VW out by the sidewalk next to the road.

"Dad," she calls. My youngest, a 22-year-old blonde waitress, she's standing in the middle of the dark, busted-up asphalt lot. "Dad, come here, Molly saw Jake's car on the news. Hurry, they're running it over and over on the DVR."

The blue-haired girl's got the bartender playing a news story over and over on Channel 4. It's a crime scene, one of the big malls southeast of town. A guy's being interviewed. In the background, over his shoulder as he talks, there, pulling up to a stop sign next to a pond in front of Barnes and Noble, is Molly and Jake's Camry, red, no mistake about it. It's Jake and Jack.

"Waterford Lakes, for fuck's sake!" Eve shouts, and she clacks Molly's beer with her own like something happy happened. The two girls lean in and talk, but I can't hear them through the music and smoke.

I can feel in my pocket that Meg's calling back. Eve's pouring me more PBR, Molly's in tears again, blue-haired girl and friends just departed, it's well after midnight, and I'm thinking, "Okay so what now?" The place is louder than ever. I lean back and raise the mug to my mouth. Maybe if Meg came, we could dance.

13 PERFECTION

JOHN KING

Crocodile World, South Orlando

The jaws of Crocodile World yawned towards Orange Blossom Trail. Two glass doors in the back of its throat let tourists out and in. Obese tourists, greasy with sweat. Sunburned nymphettes fussing with the straps of their tank tops. Hordes of yammering school-brats in matching yellow tees.

Heywood loved working here, as maintenance personnel. Walking out along the planks after the entrance, he was entirely surrounded by reptilian grace. The adolescent crocs sunbathing like perpetual spring break. The adult crocodile pond with a concrete island, fringed with a powder blue abutment, like a Riviera resort. Those floating presences in the show area.

Heywood loved the feel of Crocodile World: the real country music—soulful, lively, sincere—twanging from the loudspeakers. The architecture, as if some outpost building in the Florida Keys was transplanted to Brazil. The buoyant clomp of his boots on the wood planks.

He was en route to the white alligator cabana on a call when he stopped a moment past the show pen, by the photography station. Crystal, the 17-year-old who posed the tourists for pictures, was crouched down before a family, a mid-sized python slumped over her shoulders as she held up a baby croc, its mouth sealed with black tape, towards their eager laps.

Crystal's auburn hair was twisted into a bun. Beneath the swirls of the bottom fringes of her hair, over the curled U-shape of the serpent's middle, a skull tattoo gazed back at Heywood. He smiled, like always.

The loudspeakers crackled, the good country music switching to the *Deliverance* banjo duel / "Devil Went Down to Georgia" / "Sweet Child O' Mine" mash-up that signaled the start of the Crocky Chomparoo show. Tourists were suddenly crowding the fence like it was the Roman Coliseum. On a platform 200 feet above them, tourists who had paid their additional fees were strapping their helmets on, securing their faceguards, weighing themselves on the scale. A Crocodile World attendant in safari gear was fastening the bungees to the first two tourists. In the stage area below, two attendants in loose bib overalls flung chicken carcasses into the water, where a confusion of toothy snouts splashed.

Out of there. Heywood walked to the footpath that was the traffic spine for most of the park, this sidewalk with undulating blue swirls painted down the middle, this wave spanning the whole length of the path. On the way, he looked a moment at the tiny baby crocs in the observation chamber, looking uncannily perfect, like sculptures among the roots. In the soil on the left side of the tank, the remnants of eggs that they had emerged from.

"Yahoo!" screamed a tourist from afar, his cord going tight.

Heywood clomped forward into the white gator cabana, a wooden hut with four glass enclosures. There were polished wooden floors for its rare inhabitants, flanked with ferns and fake trees. Behind the floors were little pools, with painted dioramas of swamps offering a distorted sense of depth, as if these alligators, found in Louisiana in the 1980s, were at home, and not in claustrophobic captivity. The cabana sound system emitted groaning cicadas, twittering birds, and indigestive frogs. The bleached ridges of the alligator's unimaginably thick skin gleamed under the gentle lights. It was like getting to see a unicorn: special, but sad. Their blue eyes barely blinked.

Heywood set his tools down between the two far glass walls. He grabbed the bench's seat, which wobbled. With a ratchet and miniature flashlight, he lay on his back and squeezed underneath the seat. He could hear people walking inside the cabana, gasping with a slight sense of awe. He put the socket of the wrench around the bolts that held the seat in place, and twisted them tight, each twist adding a little metallic wheezing echo to the ambiance of the piped-in swamp sounds.

Heywood could feel a headache coming on, the start of something intense, although now it only felt big and dull, like a tennis ball perpetually bouncing off his frontal lobe. He could hear footfalls going out, footfalls in.

When Heywood slid out from the bench, he could see (through two angled layers of glass) long, pale, freckly legs, a dragonfly tattoo across an anklebone. Crystal's auburn hair.

"Oh, hi," she said. "Is the bench fixed?"

"Yeah," said Heywood.

"Can I sit there?" she asked. "I'm on break."

"Be my guest," said Heywood, with an inviting swoop of his arm.

Crystal flopped down, legs together, leaning back with her arms grabbing the back of the seat. Heywood put the ratchet back into his kit. He tried not to stare at her legs. Would it look creepy if he looked at her face?

"I love it in here," she said.

"Me, too," said Heywood.

He looked down at Crystal's face: her eyes were hard as tears dripped down her cheek. Heywood sat down next to her.

"Hey," he said.

"It's just—" she said.

("Woooooo hoooooo," went two distant tourists, with a murky, wild dopplering of echoes, and the applause of the spectators sounded like rain.)

"Go on," said Heywood.

"My boyfriend," said Crystal, "I just don't know if—"

"Go on," said Heywood.

"I don't know you very well," she said, leaning forward, scraping the tears from her face.

"That is true," said Heywood, leaning back.

"You are a rare gentleman, Hey," she said, and her lips grazed his cheek before she hustled out of the cabana.

Every atom a perfection.

Heywood stood up. His next call was the bathrooms backstage at the croc wrestling show, but instead he turned left on the boardwalk leading to the breeding marsh. Behind him, over the brush, two more tourists let go of the platform and plummeted towards the mouths of crocodiles as Axl Rose trilled like a siren. The marsh was the only place in Crocodile World where the crocs got to live in a real, if limited, environment. Here, the tall pines and the cicada songs were real. The sun beamed hotness onto the 200 yards of glinting pond.

It was time. Heywood lifted himself onto the railing, and stood upright. There were at least a dozen crocodiles in this water. In the shadow his body made, Heywood could see a school of carp swimming gently—gills flexing out, then in—near a nine-foot-long crocodile floating with its nose just atop the surface, and the most patient eyes he had ever seen. Heywood stepped forward, placing one foot on the safety extension of the fence, and then took one more step, to see what would happen next.

14 FURIOSO

MARK PURSELL

The Parliament House, South Orlando

Tonight, I'm Rosalind.

Earlier today, I was Thierry, my black MAC shirt stuck to my back, weaving around flocks of skeletal housewives and fanny-pack-wearing British tourists as they veered through the Mall at Millennia. Earlier today, I dusted Midnight Rendezvous onto the lids of a geriatric Indian woman in a sari and argued with a spaghetti-strapped *chola* about her skin tone, but all the while, the hours were accumulating and compressing beneath me, forming a springboard to vault me into Friday night. Into six-inch heels and a dark wig and a corset. Into Rosalind. Into the Parliament House.

The Parliament House on a Friday night after rain gleams and glitters and pulses. It's a dying star flinging its last desperate scraps of radiation into the night, beacons for us satellites seeking a sun to crash into. And crash into it we do, the old leather daddies with their lank ponytails—hair unwashed, yes, but harnesses supple and wet under the blacklights—and the 35-year-olds with the bodies and haircuts and teeth and clothes of 18-year-olds, a youthful varnish it takes all their leisure hours to maintain. Asians form a tight, yellow-shirted knot in the middle of the empty dance floor, electrons clustering around an unseen nucleus.

It's barely 9:30. Things aren't hopping yet.

A Britney Spears song remixed to the point of unrecognizibility cascades from the speakers, reverberating through every crossbeam and flickering light. Thirty-five years of smoke hang in the air.

Bears and otters stare vacantly across the room from the bar. Rather, their stares *appear* vacant, but really they're noticing every infinitesimal mote of cologne and eye shadow, every underwear strap.

A go-go dancer—a straight man, a brunette gym god who works out instead of working, who undoubtedly wears ratty boxers at home but here wears a red bikini brief that laces up the front—leans on the all-but-deserted bar, buying a drink for a drag queen. *The* drag queen. The closed door herself. Prosperity Jackson.

Prosperity is an institution older than the Parliament House, though her age is disguised by the pancake makeup over dusky skin, the wide span of shadow spreading from her eyes up across her temples like purple wings. She gives me a barely tolerant smile as I walk over, white teeth in a ruby-red mouth. Some people say she's a mixed-race Italian who came to Florida as a teenager on a foreign-exchange program and never went back. Others say she's from Ocala, where her family runs one of the county's oldest continually operating meth labs out in the national forest. Regardless, in this place, she is the goddess. And she's in charge of booking new talent for the Parliament House's stage shows.

Before I can help myself, I cock a hip and blurt, "Buy you a drink?" even though I've just witnessed the go-go boy—I think his name is Javier—do so, and that cocktail has been in her hand less than thirty seconds, the meniscus of Grey Goose at the top still threatening to overflow the plastic cup.

Before I can correct my mistake—how would I?—Prosperity raises an eyebrow and holds up her cup, then lifts the thin red straw to her lips. This isn't a toast, though. The way the air feels between us, it might as well be a dismissal. The cup glimmers faintly red in the light, threads of cranberry running through the vodka like nerves through tissue.

She takes a long drag on the straw. "Thierry," Prosperity says.

It's insulting to address queens by their "real" names when they're in drag, but apparently this social norm only applies to "established" queens. "Rosalind" is, at present, nobody. I'm trying to change that, but the most efficient vector for that change is Prosperity, and as closed doors go, she's padlocked to hell. I shake off the insult and feint in a different direction.

"Javier," I purr at the dancer. "Having a good night so far?"

The dancer glances at Prosperity, some uncertain expression flickering across his face. "My name is

Randall," he says (with a Southern accent, unexpected) and leaves.

Prosperity stops laughing long before the embarrassment firing through me sputters and dies. "Oh, baby," she says. "It's not even 9:30 and you already burned."

I straighten my posture, trying to inject regality into my bearing, a hint of superiority into my eyes, a little something—anything—to gain control of the conversation, but Prosperity doesn't give me the chance. She has a show to emcee at 10:00, and she undoubtedly has a different wig to put on and a quick change to choreograph. She flicks a dollar at the bartender and delicately snaps shut her velveteen clutch.

"Look, baby," she says, brushing strands of wig from her face, "you are persistent. But Miss Prosperity's patience is wearing as thin as those pantyhose you've got on. It's time for you to hear the speech that every director gives to every wannabe in every movie about said wannabe's rise to stardom. I told you: book some spots at some of the other clubs around town and work on your performance. I got baby queens beating my door down. Natasha Khan tried to buy me a flat-screen TV! And yes, baby, your makeup is *flawless*, but on stage, you're green. You're the Green Lantern. You're the Jolly Green Giant. You're *Gainesville* Green, understand me?" Suddenly, she forgoes the straw and tosses the rest of her drink back. "Work on your shit, and don't bother me again until spring, at least." She drops her cup in the trash, saunters away.

I stop her. "Prosperity."

She turns, eyes wide, a silent "What?" that couldn't be louder.

I give her what feels like a cocky smile. "I just came over to say, 'Hope you have a good show.'"

Prosperity takes that in...then laughs again. It's the only thing about her other than her Adam's apple that, even in drag, is undisguisably masculine. It's a dark, rich laugh, earth after a rainstorm. She points at me with her clutch and says, "You full of shit, baby," then turns and walks away.

■

Prosperity Jackson watches Thierry—*Rosalind*, whatever—slump in a way that's visible only to an old—no, *practiced*—queen, then heads back to the dressing room.

To anyone else, Rosalind might look the same as a few moments ago: sexy, confident, unbound. But Prosperity saw it—that slight deflation, like a day-old balloon still bouncing at the ceiling, but now listless, shrinking. Prosperity has seen it so much she catches it immediately. It's hard to see defeat in a drag queen, but not impossible. Makeup and wigs and dresses and attitude can't hide everything, no matter what some queens tell themselves.

As she walks away from Rosalind, Prosperity allows herself a flicker of sympathy for the girl, then snuffs it out. If Prosperity lit candles in her heart for every well-intentioned amateur drag queen in Orlando, her heart would be full of fire—not her own, but other people's. Prosperity played that role once, and it took years to empty herself of all the ash it left behind. There was only room for one flame in Prosperity Jackson's heart: her own.

Still, she doesn't dislike Rosalind, or any of the other baby queens clamoring at every corner for recognition, favor, performance spots. It's just that (Prosperity thinks, as she seats herself in front of her dressing room mirror, as she arrays herself in a fringed red dress and a pink pillbox hat) they don't understand yet. They don't understand that our world—this world around us, this dark universe of beautiful men and genderfuckers and revelry and mourning and sex and shallowness and joy—isn't self-contained.

If you want to know a city, visit its most infamous gay club. For reasons beyond Prosperity's understanding, a city's best or biggest or most scandalous gay club is a miniature mirror of the city it inhabits. Look at Orlando. You can see all of Orlando at Parliament: the bankers, out from under the teal pyramids of the SunTrust Building; the young "bi" boys in the first week of freshman semester at UCF; the Disney fags; the suburban power gays; the OBT junkies.

We don't live in a bubble (she steps backstage into the almost-tangible darkness of the wings, waiting for the curtain); we live in a crucible; everyone comes and brings their ghosts, too—the lover stolen in the forest and the man vanished beneath the lake, the soldier who goes down on his gun and the girl who disperses into the elements from a sun-blasted sidewalk on Colonial—they are all here. And what brings them, what binds them? The anger and madness that seethes under the world, that occasionally erupts in shattered glass and the suddenly childless. That madness is love. *Furioso*. Flames in your heart. We've all known it at one time or another, have found ourselves outcast because of it. But you are not outcast here.

Now the lights come up, and though the spot is on me and you sit in darkness, we are all mad—gleefully, ecstatically mad—together. We are a singularity. We are boundless.

15 AN EVENING UNVEILED

VANESSA BLAKESLEE

Lyman High School, Longwood

At 6:30, Meg slipped her caftan over her Romani costume, checked her lipstick in the dressing room mirror, and swished through the wings and down the hallway to the foyer of the Lyman High School auditorium. She'd been anticipating this night for weeks, her debut with the professional dance troupe, Gypsy Ishtar, her family in attendance. Well, not the *whole* family, considering the recent fiasco with Molly and Jake and their boy, Jack. But Meg's ex-husband Ned had promised to be there, at least, and he was bringing guests. When Ned had called two hours earlier, right in the middle of blocking and final run-throughs, asking if anyone had extra tickets to the sold-out show, Meg had demanded to know who else he was bringing. "Why are you being so secretive?" she implored, the phone pressed to her ear and a hand covering the other. On stage the Bollywood girls were practicing their number, half the group bouncing in saris, the other half still in yoga pants and dance tops. "Are you dating someone?

"It's not a woman," Ned replied. "It's a surprise."

Now, as she clipped down the vacant school hallway, last-minute tickets in her sweaty grasp, she tried to picture who might be waiting in the foyer with her ex. Most likely it would just be some friends of her daughter Eve's, who was also dancing in the show. How ironic, Meg thought, that it was Eve who had lured her into this whole Bellydance mother-daughter thing a couple years ago, but now Eve was stuck at the intermediate level while her mother had shimmied and undulated her way into the professional troupe. A bellydancer, at 50! Meg could hardly believe it. But she thought back to the mystery invitees. Eve's friends would be expected; Ned had mentioned a surprise.

But by the time she rounded the corner near the restrooms and spotted her ex pacing casually in front of the DVDs and hipscarves for sale, she had a decent guess of who was coming. Ned strode over, leaned down and pecked her on the cheek. "Look at you," he said, grinning. "Can't wait to see what's under that caftan." And winked.

"Like you don't already know," she said, but smiled back. Ned's presence immediately put her at ease. "So, where's Maddox? Who's he bringing?" She peered around Ned's shoulder but saw only the family and friends of her fellow dancers milling near the auditorium doors.

She'd caught Ned off-guard with her guess, she could tell by the look on his face. "Oh, you know Maddox," he replied. "Says he wants to bring some guy who works for him, a new hire who's down-and-out. Has a wife and little girl who'd enjoy the show."

"Oh," she said, adjusting one of her dangly earrings. "That's the surprise? Who's the other ticket for, then?"

"Some friend of Eve's." Ned was looking around absently. "Sienna or Indiana, something odd. She's nice. But odd." He and Meg spotted Brad, Eve's journalist-turned-dishwasher boyfriend. Ned waved him over.

"Brad!" Eve's voice bounded up the corridor. She scurried out of the hallway marked DANCERS ONLY, a silk veil wrapped over her costume; the coins underneath jingled as she ran. She grabbed Brad's arm and they kissed deeply: a bold move, Meg thought, in front of parents. "Where's Indigo?" Eve asked.

"Late, where do you think?" Brad said, rolling his eyes. Eve grabbed his hand and pressed something into his palm. "What's this?" He held up a crinkled ticket.

"For Thierry," she said. "The guy who did my make-up earlier." She tilted her face to show them. An impeccable job.

"So I'm going to have to sit through this whole show next to some dude I don't know?" Brad said, shaking his head. "You're kidding."

"Don't worry, he's a drag queen," Eve said.

The doors were open, audience members streaming into the auditorium. "Come on, we better get backstage," Meg said, nudging her daughter. "We'll see you at intermission."

Ned and Brad both said "No!" so emphatically and simultaneously, Meg's heart leapt. "Why not?" she said. "I'm going to come out and say hello to Maddox. Unless something's going on that you're not telling me?" She glanced from one to the other.

"Course not," Ned said. "It's just…why not wait until after the show? When we're all relaxed. We'll grab a drink somewhere."

"Alright," Meg said warily, turning her back. What on earth was her ex-husband up to?

■

Meg's Romani number was third in the program. On stage she was grateful for the blinding lights which made discerning individual faces nearly impossible. She loved dancing, not performing, but she'd worked too hard not to perform. Long before her fiftieth birthday she'd learned to not take for granted the years left, and even then she could feel her prime coming to an end. It was the reason she'd stuck to the slower-paced Thursday night technique class, leaving the twenty-somethings to the floor work and backbends. Even tonight, as she panted and hurried behind the curtain to the dressing room, she knew her days of performing at the professional level required of the troupe wouldn't likely extend beyond a few seasons.

How strange to think she'd spent the middle decades of her life in Orlando. But then, she loved this city, its waywardness and contradiction opening up to peculiar opportunity—like the way she'd met up with Eve that first class, stumbling into the Aloma Ave. dance studio tucked in a half-abandoned commercial strip across from a sketchy apartment complex. Who would have ever guessed Orlando boasted one of the best Middle Eastern dance schools in the United States? When a position had opened earlier that year and she'd considered moving to either Louisiana or Missouri, her co-worker Susie had warned, "You won't find a dance school like that anywhere else, except New York." Meg had turned down the offer.

But Orlando was like that. Nothing like what outsiders assumed. You just had to go out there and find it.

Meg was hurrying into her next costume, a pirate wench ensemble for the "Gypsy Saloon" number, when Eve poked her head in the dressing room. "Mom," she said. "Are you going out there for intermission?"

"I plan on it," Meg said, dabbing more blush on her cheeks. She was squeezed between the other dancers for a spot in the mirror. "Evie, you shouldn't be standing there, you're blocking traffic."

"Sorry," Eve said, wincing. "It's just that I got a good look from the wings when we were waiting to go on for our number, and I don't think Uncle Maddox brought the plumber's family."

The stage manager flung open the door, called, "Gypsies on deck!"

"Well, who did he bring?"

"Molly's there," Eve said. "And it looks like Jake and Jack are with her."

"*Molly*?" Meg said. But there was no time; the Gypsies were filing out of the dressing room. One of them hissed to Eve: "Later, and quit blocking the door!"

Meg floated after them, into her place in the wings on Stage Right. Performing didn't usually make her nervous, even in front of thousand-member audiences, but she found her legs had turned watery. Her daughter Molly, sitting with the husband who'd stolen their child and fled town? How was that possible? Had Jake contacted Maddox? Or had Ned found them somehow, against all odds, ever the peacemaker? And who on earth had thought *her* Bellydance show would be an optimal place for this reunion? *Breathe*, she told herself. *Remember, you're excited, not nervous.*

The music from the previous number, a fan dance, waned. The dancers shuffled past, a rustle of whispering congratulations, fabric and feathers. The Gypsies were on.

▪

At intermission Meg joined Eve in the hallway, and they wordlessly hurried to the packed foyer. There was Molly alongside her husband and son, her arms loose over the boy's shoulders. Maddox was there, too, standing beside Jake, who shifted uncomfortably when Meg's eyes met his. Ned, Brad, and a young man and woman with colored hair and unusual clothing moved to congratulate Eve on her veil performance, leaving Meg to confront her daughter's family.

"Well," Meg said. "Surprise, surprise. Nice you all could see the show together. I wasn't sure what to expect."

Maddox beamed. "So Ned threw you off, did he?" He laughed. "When Jake contacted me, I just couldn't resist devising this little get-together."

Meg squinted at Maddox, shook her head. She'd never been sure what to make of him, and even now he seemed to be keeping dark secrets. "I just hope it's for the best," she said. "Not too soon." Her gaze lifted and fell on Molly, but Meg's eldest daughter was expressionless, exhausted-looking; Jack and Jake appeared the same. Molly excused herself to smoke a cigarette.

"I've got to get backstage," Meg said. "But it's wonderful to see you." She nodded at Jake. "And my grandson."

Ned stepped closer, cupped Meg's arm. "We'll get together after the show," he said. "The Eden Bar, in Maitland? You know the place?"

"Sure," she said. She'd been there before, an outdoor bar with dripping Spanish moss and twinkling white lights. "See you then."

"Wait," Jack called, running after her. "Grandma, how old are you?"

"I just turned 50 this summer."

Her grandson clutched his cheeks and made a shock face. He said, his voice brimming with awe, "That's way too old for such a beautiful lady!"

■

The second act went off flawlessly, even the tricky dance with the Egyptian cane; Meg had harbored nightmares about the prop whizzing from her grasp, into the audience. Afterward, she and Eve changed.

Brad met them at Eve's car, offered to drive them to the bar so they could come down from the rush of performing. He was a quiet young man, polite, but everyone knew he was marked by the loss of his childhood friend. (It was in the papers: the fountain, the body. Everyone knew, but no one could talk about it with Brad here, even though it was Maddox's company that had pulled the body from the water.) It was a tragedy akin to her own family's mess: origins murky, answers elusive...and complications far too difficult for one night of family bonding to resolve.

But when they pulled into the Eden Bar, the lit path welcomed them to an oasis of tables. Ned, Maddox, and the others were already sitting at a table in front of a bubbling fountain. "Perfect, isn't it?" Ned called as Meg approached, pulled out the chair beside him. He leaned back, opened his palms to the sky and said, "You can't get more perfect than this."

ABOUT THE AUTHORS

NATHAN HOLIC teaches writing courses at the University of Central Florida, where he serves as the Graphic Narrative Editor at *The Florida Review*. His fiction has appeared in *The Apalachee Review*, *The Portland Review*, and *The Roanoke Review*, and his serialized graphic narrative "Clutter" (a fictional story set in Orlando, and structured as a home décor catalogue) appears at the online magazine *Smalldoggies*. Like most other Orlando residents, he is from somewhere else.

GENE ALBAMONTE graduated with an MFA in Creative Writing from the University of Central Florida. He was one of thirty writers accepted to the 2010 Sirenland Writers Conference, where he studied under Dani Shapiro—editor of *Best New American Voices 2010*. Thus far, his fiction has appeared or is forthcoming in *Monkeybicycle*, *Southern Indiana Review*, *The Rattling Wall*, *Used Furniture Review* and *Clapboard House*. He also has a story published in *Fragmentation + Other Stories*—a collection of short stories featuring Florida writers published by Burrow Press. Another story of his was named one of the top 25 in *Glimmer Train*'s January 2008 Family Matters competition, earning a Finalist position. He also had a story earn an Honorable Mention position in *Glimmer Train*'s April 2008 Family Matters competition. Gene currently writes a weekly humor column called "Gallimaufry" for *PANK Magazine*'s blog.

CHRIS WIEWIORA has lived in Orlando since 1996 and worked on *The Florida Review* while attending the University of Central Florida. He lives in Ames, IA, where he is an MFA candidate at Iowa State University's Creative Writing and Environment program. His fiction has appeared on *A cappella Zoo*, *YouMustBeThisTalltoRide.net*, *SmokeLong Quarterly*, *The Planet Formerly Known as Earth*, and *The Quotable*. But he mostly writes nonfiction. Read more at chriswiewiora.com.

J. BRADLEY is a contributing writer to *Specter Magazine* and the Interviews Editor of *PANK Magazine*. He is the author of *Bodies Made of Smoke* (HOUSEFIRE, 2011) and the upcoming fiction/poetry collection, *We Will Live Like Our Ghosts Will Live* (YesYes Books, 2013). J. Bradley lives at iheartfailure.net.

DAN SINCLAIR spent about a third of his life living in Orlando. During that time, he had his Acura Integra GS-R stolen from out front of his apartment and earned an MFA from the University of Central Florida. He now resides in Los Angeles, trying to be some kind of professional writer. Through his primary focus is television and film, he also writes for an indie music site (theheardproject.com), tries to make people laugh with his blog (thingsbadhappen.com/thislifepathetic), and hopes to someday finish his novel (sigh).

HUNTER CHOATE lives and writes in Orlando. His work has appeared in *elimae*, *Word Riot*, *Fragmentation + Other Stories*, and others. Find him online at hunterchoate.com.

Too quick across the face of this earth, TOM DEBEAUCHAMP has never watched a puppy grow up to a dog and die. His stories and reviews have appeared here and there, online and in print. He waits for mail that never comes. He attracts sometimes the inverse of moths and jars them and stores them in cool, damp, dark places where they batter the glass with their bodies, desperate to touch the unity for which inverse moths despair. He reminds you we are all closer always to the molten central fire than we'll ever be to the distant radiations of space. His most recent attempt at a web site is the following: softsolids.tumblr.com.

JAY HAFFNER is an English teacher and Newspaper advisor at a local Orlando high school. He is a former editor for both *The Cypress Dome* and *The Florida Review*, and now spends his time trying to convince teenagers that things like reading and writing will actually get them dates in college. He is a native of Detroit, and though he has lived in Florida for many years, he has never been able to tan.

ASHLEY INGUANTA is an Orlando-based writer and photographer who earned her MFA from the University of Central Florida. Her writing and photography have appeared in magazines such as *SmokeLong Quarterly*, *Make/Shift Magazine*, *Pindeldyboz*, *Sweet: A Literary Confection*, *Gone Lawn*, *Wigleaf*, and *Redivider*. This year, she also earned an honorable mention in *Glimmer Train* for their Very Short Fiction Award. Keep up to date with her publications and travels at ashleyinguanta.com.

CHRIS HEAVENER is the editor of *Annalemma Magazine*: annalemma.net.

JARED SILVIA is a writer, probably.

LINDSAY HUNTER grew up in Orlando and now lives in Chicago, where she co-hosts the Quickies! reading series. Her work has been published widely online and in print, and her first book, *Daddy's*, is out now on *f*eatherproo*f* books. Find her at lindsayhunter.com.

PHILIP F. DEAVER is Professor of English and Writer in Residence at Rollins College. He also teaches on the fiction and poetry faculties in the Spalding University brief residency MFA program. Deaver writes and publishes in fiction, creative nonfiction, and poetry genres, with books available on Amazon. He's won the Flannery O'Connor Award for Short Fiction and held fellowships from the National Endowment for the Arts and Bread Loaf Writers Conference. His story collection *Silent Retreats* was recently released in a Kindle version. He's currently working on a set of long short stories with an international flavor.

JOHN KING, an aficionado of college degrees, recently acquired his fourth, an MFA in creative writing from NYU. While his doppelganger proudly teaches composition and creative writing at the University of Central Florida, John currently resides at an undisclosed location and toils on his epic novel, *Guy Psycho and the Ziggurat of Shame*. He also reviews books for *The Literary Review* and theater for *Shakespeare Bulletin*. His work has appeared in *Turnrow*, *Gargoyle*, and *Pearl*, and is forthcoming from *Palooka*.

MARK PURSELL has served as an intern and later the poetry editor at *The Florida Review*. His work has appeared in *The New Orleans Review* and *Nimrod International Journal*. He currently teaches writing courses at Full Sail University.

VANESSA BLAKESLEE studied creative writing at Rollins College and the University of Central Florida before earning the MFA in Writing at Vermont College of Fine Arts. Her work has appeared in *The Southern Review*, *New York Quarterly*, *The Bellingham Review*, *Green Mountains Review*, *Southern Poetry Review*, *The Paris Review Daily*, and dozens more in print and online. Her award-winning short fiction has been recognized by grants and fellowships from Yaddo, the Ragdale Foundation, the Atlantic Center for the Arts, and the Virginia Center for the Creative Arts, among others. Vanessa is also a Master-level bellydancer at Orlando Bellydance School of Middle Eastern Dance and has performed veil, sword, zill, Romani, and assaya (Egyptian cane) routines. Find Vanessa online at vanessablakeslee.com.

www.ingramcontent.com/pod-product-compliance
Lightning Source LLC
Chambersburg PA
CBHW030645190726
48286CB00008B/2667

* 9 7 8 1 9 4 1 6 8 1 0 7 7 *